Wavy Scissors Art

Use wavy-edge scissors to create terrific designs and accents from paper. With this book you'll find hours of fun projects for scrapbook pages, cards, stationery, bulletin boards, kid crafts and much more!

Holiday Scrapbook Page
⅝" circle punch, Scallop and Jumbo Scallop scissors, Letter Stickers

Violets Stationery Page -
³⁄₁₆" star punch, 1¹⁄₁₆" circle template, Pompeii Canyon cutters and Jumbo Scallop scissors

'Thank You' Card - 4⅞" x 7¼" piece of White paper, 5" x 7¼" piece of parchment paper, Jumbo Scallop scissors, Flowers, Leaves, Letter stickers

Gift Tag - 2¼" x 3½" piece of parchment paper, 2⅛" x 3¼" piece of White paper, Jumbo Scallop scissors, Flowers, Leaves, Marker, ⅛" hole punch, Cord

Table of Contents

Straight Scissors - Use a pencil to draw light guidelines on the back of paper. Cut along guideline.

Wavy Scissors - Turn wavy edge scissors over to cut a second and different design. Create more designs by aligning scissor cuts in different ways. Cut a border or strip by making a second cut parallel to the first cut forming a mirror image. Cut other designs by shifting or misaligning the blade pattern on the second cut. For a continuous design, align scissors blade design with the previous cut. Do not cut to the very end of the blades.

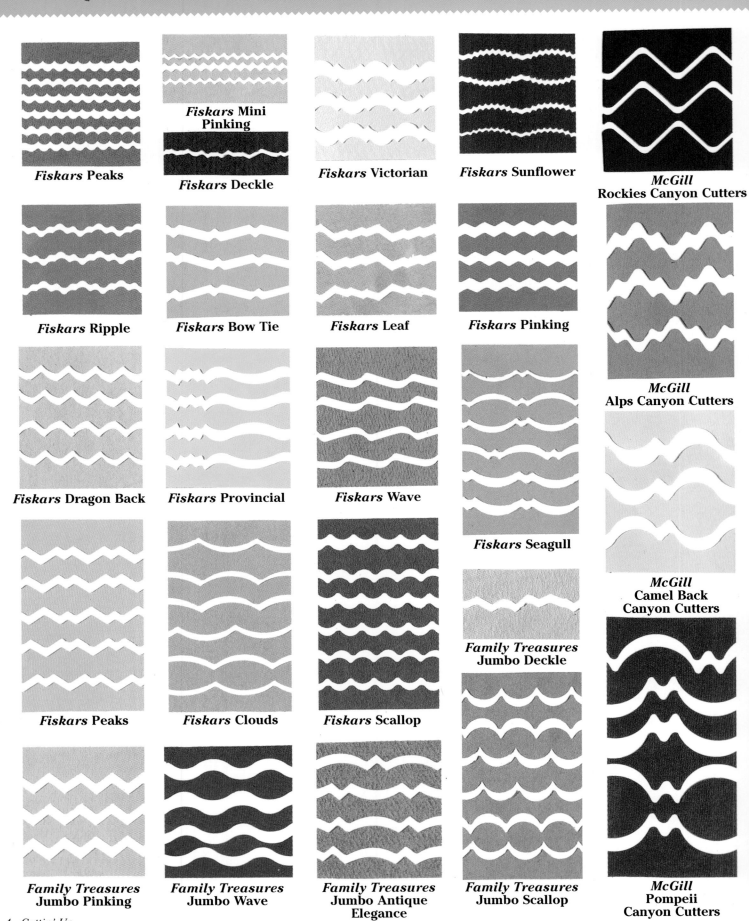

Wavy Scissors

Wavy edge scissors are the beginning of creativity! Each wavy edge can create several looks. Don't be afraid to substitute different edges.

Fiskars Peaks

Fiskars Mini Pinking

Fiskars Deckle

Fiskars Victorian

Fiskars Sunflower

McGill Rockies Canyon Cutters

Fiskars Ripple

Fiskars Bow Tie

Fiskars Leaf

Fiskars Pinking

McGill Alps Canyon Cutters

Fiskars Dragon Back

Fiskars Provincial

Fiskars Wave

Fiskars Seagull

McGill Camel Back Canyon Cutters

Fiskars Peaks

Fiskars Clouds

Fiskars Scallop

Family Treasures Jumbo Deckle

Family Treasures Jumbo Pinking

Family Treasures Jumbo Wave

Family Treasures Jumbo Antique Elegance

Family Treasures Jumbo Scallop

McGill Pompeii Canyon Cutters

How to Use Wavy Scissors

Start with Basic edges like the Scallop and Pinking wavy edges. It is easy to create hundreds of shapes with just these basics. Add a couple more edges as you make more designs. Remember, you can always substitute a different edge to create a different and sometimes better look!

Wavy-Edge Scissors are fun to use. Create inexpensive borders and designs from acid-free colored cardstock, paper and decorative ScrapHappy™ papers.

Ease in Cutting. Use a piece of paper about the size of the object to be cut.

End of Scissors. Do not cut to the tip of scissors. Stop just short of the end to avoid rough edges and to keep scissors ends from locking.

Two for One. Turn scissors over to make two different design edges.

Circles & Shapes. Move paper and hold the scissors steady when cutting out shapes and circles.

Two-Way or Tube Glue. Apply glue to a very tiny area. Arrange small pieces using tweezers.

Two-Way or Tube Glue. Squeeze a small amount of glue on cardboard or a plastic drink lid, then use a corsage pin to apply glue to very tiny areas.

Paper Strips. Very thin strips of paper will curve when glued down for stems. Cardstock is easier to cut into very thin strips because it has more body than regular paper.

'Boo-Boos'. Use sharp straight edge scissors to round small snags or to smooth rough edges. Sometimes small paper burrs can be removed with a fingernail emery board.

Cut Straight Lines. Draw light guidelines on the back of the cardstock or paper with a pencil. Cut with the wavy scissors lined up against the guideline.

Paper Trimmer. For straight lines, a paper trimmer is a wonderful tool. It can both cut and score.

Circle & Oval Cutter. As an option to cutting with scissors, a cutting tool is a wonderful aid. Cut a circle larger than needed, then trim around the edges with wavy scissors.

Magnetic Dolls

Simple Dolls - Just use the basic patterns on pages 8-9 to cut out and glue dolls to pages.

Magnetic Dolls - These dolls are fun to use in your scrapbook. All the clothes are interchangeable, so dolls can be dressed and redressed over and over. To protect magnetic clothes, laminate a clear cover on the top side. Magnets are great because they will work right through page protectors. Have Fun!

"Tigger our kitty loves to drink warm milk."

"Baby Ryan loves his little bear."

"Janie loves to wear blue."

Simple Dolls - Make dolls following cutting and punching instructions on pages 8 and 9. Trace clothing patterns on pages 6-7. Cut out and glue. Draw details with markers.

Magnetic Dolls - Cut sheet magnet to fit the back of body and a strip for clothes. Before gluing magnet to the back of clothes and body, test to see if the magnet is positioned correctly or needs to be turned over.

Jointed Bear - Cut body pieces for bear. Glue head to body. Use marker to draw the face. Punch a 1/16" hole in body where arms and legs attach. Punch a 1/16" hole in the top of each arm and leg. Punch 8 'buttons' using a 1/4" circle punch. Use a needle to make 2 holes in each 'button'. Cut a 6" piece of heavy thread. Insert one thread end down through each hole in a 'button'. Bring ends together and insert through hole in body, then through hole in arm. Separate thread ends and insert one end through each hole in second 'button'. Tie a knot. Repeat for remaining arm and legs.

Pantaloons, Slip - Mini scallop scissors, Pink marker
Sun Suit - Mini scallop scissors, Black marker
Jeans - Mini pinking scissors, Orange marker
T-shirt - Mini scallop scissors, Red marker
Leotard - Mini scallop and bow tie scissors
Green Dress - Ripple and bow tie scissors
Pink Dress - Mini scallop, scallop and bow tie scissors
Pajamas - Mini scallop scissors, Black marker
Cat's Vest, Shorts - Mini scallop scissors, Black marker
Girl's Sundress - Scallop and mini scallop scissors
Jointed Bear's Diaper - 1 1/2" oval template, Black marker
Bear's Bikini - Mini scallop and pinking scissors
Boy's Shirt, Overalls - Mini pinking scissors, Orange marker
Rabbit's Vest, Tie - Mini scallop and bow tie scissors, Black marker.

"Suzy's favorite toy is a cuddly little bear."

"Tommy loves Sir Bunny. He carries him everywhere."

Redhead Boy - ⁵⁄₁₆" and 1¼" circle punches, ⁷⁄₈" circle template, Pinking, Scallop and Bow Tie scissors

Baby - ⅛", ¼", ⅝" and 1¼" circle punches, 1¼" circle template, Jumbo Scallop and Bow Tie scissors

Girl/Yellow Bow - ¾" heart punch, 1¼" circle punch, 1¼" circle template, Scallop and Bow Tie scissors

Crew Cut Boy - ¼", ⁵⁄₁₆" and 1¼" circle punches, Pinking scissors

Blonde Girl - 1¼" circle punch, ⁷⁄₈" circle template, Jumbo Scallop, Bow Tie and Scallop scissors

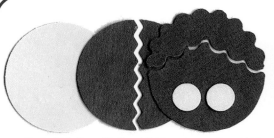

Curly Hair Boy - ⁵⁄₁₆" and 1¼" circle punches, 1¼" circle template, Pinking and Scallop scissors

Redhead Girl - 1¼" circle punch, 1⅜" and 1¼" circle templates, Jumbo Scallop and Bow Tie scissors

Black Hair Boy - ⁵⁄₁₆" and 1¼" circle punches, 1¼" circle template, Mini Pinking, Mini Scallop and Bow Tie scissors

Pigtail Girl - 1¼" circle punch, Jumbo Scallop, Bow Tie and Jumbo Pinking scissors

Friends - ³⁄₁₆" and ¾" heart punches, ⁵⁄₁₆" and 1¼" circle punches, ⅝" and 1¼" circle templates, Jumbo Scallop, Mini Scallop and Bow Tie scissors

Doll Faces & Bodies

"I love mom's apple pie."

"Daddy's little angel."

"I love to go fishing with my grandad."

"Happy Day!"

Paper Doll - ¼" circle punch, ⅞" circle template, Jumbo Scallop scissors. Trace patterns, cut out body and shorts.

Basic Animal Body - ⅞", 1" and 1¼" oval templates, ⅞" circle template

Bear Head - ⅞" circle template, ⅝" and ½" oval templates, ⅛" circle punch, Mini Pinking scissors

Cat Head - ⅞" circle template, ¼" triangle template, Mini Pinking scissors

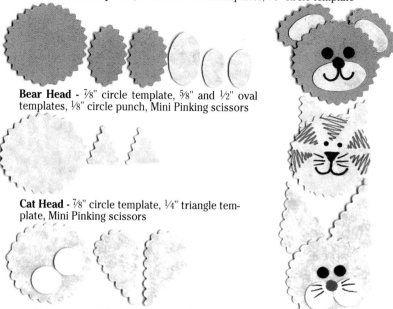

Rabbit Head - ⅞" circle template, ¾" heart template, ⅛" and ⁵⁄₁₆" circle punches, Mini Scallop scissors

Beautiful Borders

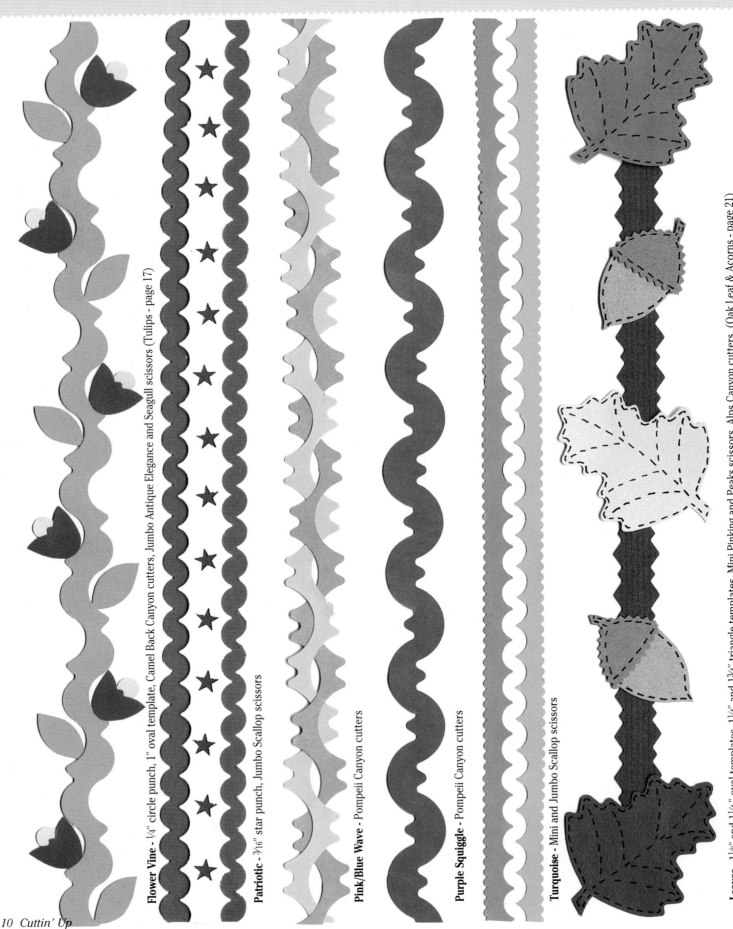

Flower Vine - ¼" circle punch, 1" oval template, Camel Back Canyon cutters, Jumbo Antique Elegance and Seagull scissors (Tulips - page 17)

Patriotic - ³⁄₁₆" star punch, Jumbo Scallop scissors

Pink/Blue Wave - Pompeii Canyon cutters

Purple Squiggle - Pompeii Canyon cutters

Turquoise - Mini and Jumbo Scallop scissors

Leaves - 1⅛" and 1¼" oval templates, 1¼" and 1¾" triangle templates, Mini Pinking and Peaks scissors, Alps Canyon cutters (Oak Leaf & Acorns - page 21)

Remember, heavier cardstock makes cutting easier than regular paper.

Holly - ¼" circle punch, Scallop scissors, Camel Back Canyon cutters (Holly Leaves - page 24)

Peppermint Candy - Mini Pinking scissors, Alps and Pompeii Canyon cutters, Red marker (Candy - page 19)

Halloween - ¹⁄₁₆" circle punch, 1¹⁄₁₆" circle template, Scallop, Jumbo Scallop, Mini Pinking, Pinking and Jumbo Pinking scissors (Spider & Bat - page 23)

Peppermint Stick - Jumbo Antique Elegance scissors, Red marker

Bees - ⁵⁄₁₆" circle punch, ½" circle and ¾" oval templates, Mini Pinking and Mini Scallop scissors, Black marker (Bee - page 21)

Bountiful Borders

Use colorful borders to dress up any page or card.

Butterflies - ⅛" circle punch, ⅝" heart template, Scallop and Mini Scallop scissors, Alps Canyon cutters (Butterfly - page 20)

Gifts - ⅜" circle punch, ½" x ¾ " and ½" x 1" rectangle templates, ½" square template, Mini Scallop, Scallop and Bow Tie scissors (Gifts - page 25)

Pink Lace - ¼" x ¾ " heart punch, Mini Scallop scissors, Pompeii Canyon cutters

Apples - ⅝ " circle punch, Mini Pinking and Peaks scissors Apples - page 27)

Birdhouses - ¼ " circle punch, ¼ " circle template, ½" and ¾ " heart templates, ⅞ " oval template, ⅜" x ¾" rectangle template, Mini Scallop scissors, Alps Canyon cutters, Crimper (Birdhouses - page 19)

Lacy Hearts - ¹⁄₁₆" circle punch, ⅞" heart punch, 1" heart template, Victorian and Scallop scissors (Hearts - page 18)

Turquoise/Magenta Twist - Rockies Canyon cutters

Be creative! Mix solid color papers and small pattern papers for a really special look.

Black/Gold - Jumbo Scallop scissors

Violets - 3/16" star punch, 3/4" circle template, Jumbo Scallop scissors, Alps Canyon cutters (Basic Flowers - page 17)

Navy/Red Hearts - Using Jumbo Scallop scissors, cut a strip of Red paper. Move over 1/8", make an identical cut to make a swag design. Repeat using Navy paper. Place strips with points touching, weave every other Navy point under a Red point and glue. Cut and glue a Navy scalloped strip behind Red hearts.

Crabs - 1/16" circle punch, 1/2" star punch, 1 1/16" circle template, Mini Pinking, Jumbo Pinking, Jumbo Wave and Cloud scissors (Crab - page 23)

Tulips - Alps and Rockies Canyon cutters

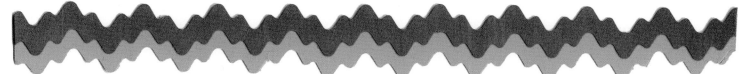

Red/Green Wave - Alps Canyon cutters

Blue Swag - 7/16" and 3/4" heart punches, Jumbo Wave scissors, Pompeii Canyon cutters

Creative Matting

Use wavy edge scissors to crop photos into geometric shapes. Make people the focal point of the photo by cutting away uninteresting backgrounds. Cut mats from paper using wavy edge scissors. Plan ahead to make the wavy scissors design match in all 4 corners of the mat. Cut a straight strip with wavy edge scissors. Place the strip on the mat along one edge. Adjust the strip to make the corner design you want. Trace design and cut out. Glue cropped photo on top of mat.

Pumpkin - 3½" oval template, 2" circle template, Scallop and Jumbo Pinking scissors, Alps canyon cutters (Leaves - page 17)

Wreath - ¾" and ⁷⁄₁₆" heart punches, ¼" circle punch, 1 ¾" and 3" circle templates, Scallop and Jumbo Wave scissors

Gift - ¾" and ⁷⁄₁₆" heart punches, 2" circle and 3" square templates, Mini Scallop scissors

Basket - ¾" and ⁷⁄₁₆" heart punches, ¾" and 3" oval templates, Mini Scallop scissors, crimper

Heart -
1/8" circle punch, 1/4" star punch, 3 1/2" heart template, 5/8" circle template, Scallop and Jumbo Scallop scissors

Beach -
1/16" circle punch, 5/8" circle template, Mini Pinking, Jumbo Pinking and Jumbo Wave scissors, Camel Back Canyon cutters (Crab - page 23)

Apple - 1/16" circle punch, 1 1/2", 2" and 3 1/4" circle templates, 1 1/4" heart template, Mini Scallop and Scallop scissors

Baby -
2 1/4", 2 3/4" and 3" circle templates, Mini Scallop, Jumbo Scallop and Bow Tie scissors

Oval -
1/8" circle punch, 4" oval template, Mini Scallop scissors, Pompeii Canyon cutters

Fanciful Flowers

Grace a Garden with colorful flowers, butterflies, and bees. Use wavy scissors to create a garden of delight with basic colored paper.

"Flowers cut from assorted colors of paper really dress up scrapbook pages and greeting cards.."

Make this...into →

Small Turquoise Flower - ⅛" circle punch, ⅝" oval template, ⅜", ⅝" and ⅞" circle templates, Scallop and Mini Pinking scissors

Large Turquoise Flower - 5⁄16" circle punch, ¾" oval template, 1¹⁄16", 1⅛" and 1½" circle templates, Jumbo Scallop and Mini Pinking scissors

Make this...into →

Small Pink Flower - ¼" circle punch, ⁷⁄16", 1¹⁄16" and 1" circle templates, Mini Pinking and Pinking scissors, Alps Canyon cutters

Large Pink Flower - 5⁄16" circle punch, 1¹⁄16", 1⅛" and 1½" circle templates, Mini Pinking, Pinking and Jumbo Pinking scissors, Alps Canyon cutters

Grass - Sunflower scissors

Red Flower - ¼" circle punch, ¼" and ⅞" circle templates, Mini Pinking and Pinking scissors, Alps Canyon cutters

Blue Bells - ¼" circle punch, 1" oval template, Mini Pinking and Seagull scissors

Magenta Flower - ¼" circle punch, ⅝" and ⅞" circle templates, ⅝" oval template, Scallop and Mini Pinking scissors

16 *Cuttin' Up*

"Sunflowers are symbols of joy and happy days."

Simple Shapes turn into ➞

Small Blackeyed Susan - ¼" circle punch, ⅜" and ⅞" circle templates, 1¾" oval template, Mini Scallop and Scallop scissors

Large Blackeyed Susan - ⅜", 9/16" and 1½" circle templates, 2" oval template, Mini Scallop and Jumbo Scallop scissors

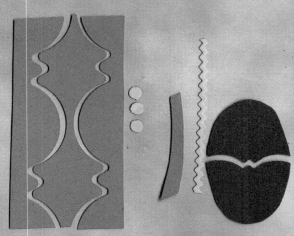

Turn leaves and petals into ➞

Small Tulip - ⅛" circle punch, 1¼" oval template, Seagull and Mini Pinking scissors, Pompeii Canyon cutters

Large Tulip - ¼" circle punch, 2¼" oval template, Mini Pinking scissors, Pompeii Canyon cutters

Orange Flower - 5/16" circle punch, ⅞" and 1" circle templates, 1 7/16" oval template, Scallop and Mini Pinking scissors

Turquoise Star - ¼" star punch, ⅝" and ⅞" circle templates, Pinking and Mini Pinking scissors, Pompeii Canyon cutters

Violets - 3/16" star punch, ¾" oval template, 1 1/16" circle template, Mini Pinking and Jumbo Scallop scissors

Fence - Cut one long edge of a 3" x 5" piece of White paper with Jumbo Pinking scissors, cut pickets using pinked edge as a guide.

Scissors Designs

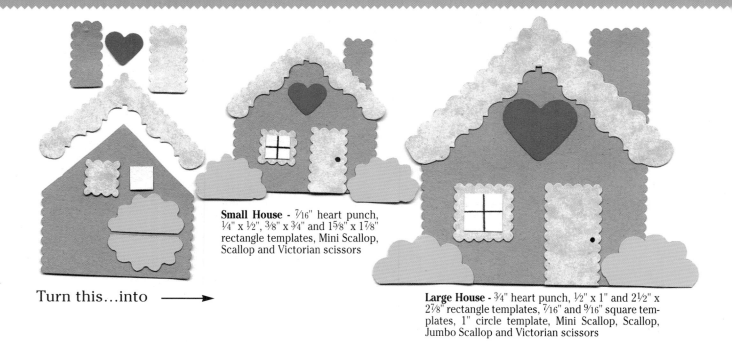

Turn this...into ➔

Small House - ⁷⁄₁₆" heart punch, ¼" x ½", ³⁄₈" x ¾" and 1⁵⁄₈" x 1⁷⁄₈" rectangle templates, Mini Scallop, Scallop and Victorian scissors

Large House - ¾" heart punch, ½" x 1" and 2½" x 2⁷⁄₈" rectangle templates, ⁷⁄₁₆" and ⁹⁄₁₆" square templates, 1" circle template, Mini Scallop, Scallop, Jumbo Scallop and Victorian scissors

Turn this...into ➔

Small Banana Split - ⅛" circle punch, ½" oval punch, ½" circle template, 1⅝" oval template, Mini Scallop and Scallop scissors

Large Banana Split - ¼" circle punch, ⅝" and 3" oval templates, ¾" circle template, Scallop and Jumbo Scallop scissors

Turn this...into ➔

Small Lacy Hearts - ¹⁄₁₆" circle punch, ¾" and 1¼" heart punches, 1" and 1½" heart templates, Scallop scissors

Large Lacy Hearts - ⅛ circle punch, 1½", 1¾", 2¼" and 2½" heart templates, Jumbo Scallop scissors

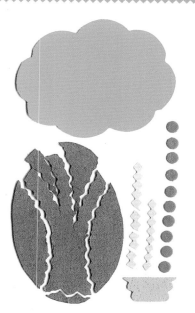

"Apple trees, pear trees and peach trees make great accents in every color."

Turn this...into ➞

Small Apple Tree - ⅛" circle punch, 1¼" oval template, Mini Pinking, Mini Scallop, Deckle and Cloud scissors

Large Apple Tree - ¼" circle punch, 2½" oval template, Mini Scallop, Pinking, Deckle and Cloud scissors

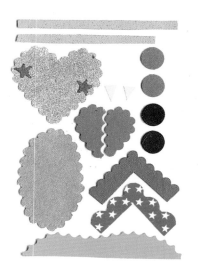

Turn this...into ➞

Small Birdhouses - ¼" circle punch, ¾" heart template, ⅞" oval template, Mini Scallop and Scallop scissors

Large Birdhouses - ¼" circle punch, 1¼" oval template, ¾" and 1¼" heart templates, Mini Scallop and Scallop scissors

Turn this...into ➞

Peppermint Candy - Mini Pinking scissors, Pompeii Canyon cutters, Red marker

Scissors Designs

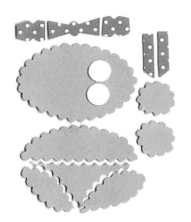

"Pink bunnies are perfect for babies. They look great in blue too."

Turn this...into ➡️

Small Rabbit - 1/8" and 1/4" circle punches, 3/8" circle template, 1 1/4" oval template, Mini Scallop and Bow Tie scissors

Large Rabbit - 1/4" circle punch, 1/2" circle template, 2 1/2" oval template, Mini Scallop, Scallop and Bow Tie scissors

"Beautiful butterflies look great in a rainbow of colors."

Turn this...into ➡️

Small Butterfly - 1/8" circle punch, 1" heart template, Mini Scallop and Scallop scissors

Large Butterfly - 1/8" circle punch, 1 3/4" heart template, Jumbo Scallop and Scallop scissors

"Sheep are farm days and counting to sleep."

Turn this...into ➡️

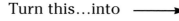

Small Sheep - 7/16" heart punch, 1 1/4" oval template, Jumbo Scallop scissors, 3/16" x 3/8" strips

Large Sheep - 3/4" heart punch, 2 1/4" oval template, Jumbo Scallop scissors, 1/4" x 1/2" strips

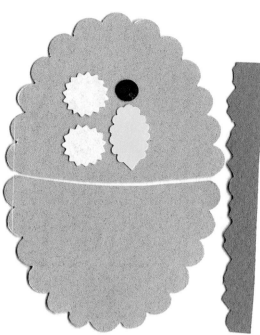

Turn this...into ➝

"Buzz around... Buzz around... Be my little honey bee."

Beehive and Bees- ¼" circle punch, ⅝" and 3¼" oval templates, ⅜" circle template, Mini Scallop, Jumbo Scallop, Mini Pinking and Jumbo Deckle scissors, Brown and Black markers

"I love mom's cherry pie. It is really yummy."

Turn this...into ➝

Small Cherries - ⁵⁄₁₆" and ⅝" circle punches, ¾" heart template, Mini Pinking scissors

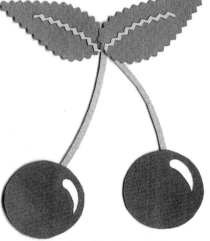

Large Cherries - ⅝" and ⅞" circle punches, 1¼" heart template, Mini Pinking scissors

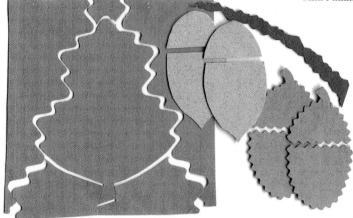

Turn this...into ➝

Acorns - 1⅛" and 1¼" oval templates, 1¾" triangle template, Mini Pinking and Deckle scissors, Alps Canyon cutters

Scissors Designs

"Crosses are great for sweet thoughts and sentiments."

Turn this...into →

Small Cross - 1/16" and 1/8" circle punches, 3/16" heart punch, Mini Scallop and Jumbo Wave scissors

Large Cross - 1/16" and 1/8" circle punches, 3/16" heart punch, Jumbo Wave scissors

"Baa Baa, Black or White Sheep."

Turn this...into →

Small Lamb - 1/16", 1/8" and 5/8" circle punches, 7/16" heart punch, 1" circle template, Bow Tie and Jumbo Scallop scissors

Large Lamb - 1/16" and 1/8" circle punches, 3/4" heart punch, 7/8" and 1 1/8" circle templates, Bow Tie and Jumbo Scallop scissors

Turn this...into →

Small Sun & Clouds - 7/8" and 1 1/4" circle templates, 1 1/4" and 1 5/8" oval templates, Jumbo Pinking and Clouds scissors, Markers

Large Sun & Clouds - 1 1/2" and 2" circle templates, 2 1/4" and 2 7/8" oval templates, Jumbo Pinking and Clouds scissors, Markers

"Make a bitty black bat."

Small Bat - 1/16" circle punch, Jumbo Scallop and Scallop scissors

Turn this...into →

Large Bat - 1/16" circle punch, Jumbo Scallop scissors, Alps Canyon cutters

"Who's there? Boo, Boo Who."

Turn this...into →

Small Ghost - 1/8" circle punch, 2" oval template, Jumbo Wave scissors, Black marker

Large Ghost - 1/8" circle punch, 3" oval template, Jumbo Wave scissors, Black marker, 'BOO!' sticker

"Itsy bitsy spider."

Turn this...into →

Small Spider or Crab - 1/16" circle punch, 11/16" circle template, Mini and Jumbo Pinking scissors

Large Spider - 1/8" circle punch, 11/8" circle template, Jumbo Pinking scissors

"Pretty pumpkins."

Turn this...into →

Small Pumpkin - 1/2" and 2" circle templates, 2" oval template, Mini Scallop, Mini Pinking and Pinking scissors

Large Pumpkin - 1" and 2" circle templates, 31/4" oval template, Mini Pinking, Jumbo Pinking and Scallop scissors

Scissors Designs

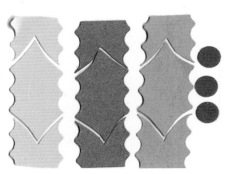

Turn this...into →

"Happy holly days."

Small Holly - ¼" circle punch, Scallop scissors

Large Holly - ⁵⁄₁₆" circle punch, Jumbo Scallop scissors

Turn this...into →

"Festive trees come in dozens of sizes and shapes."

Small Christmas Tree - ⅛" circle punch, ¼" star punch, 2" triangle template, Dragon Back scissors

Large Christmas Tree - ¼" circle punch, ½" star punch, 3" triangle template, Dragon Back scissors

Turn this...into →

"Angels watching over you and me."

Small Angel - ¹⁄₁₆" and ⅝" circle punches, ³⁄₁₆" star punch, ⁷⁄₁₆" heart punch, ⅝" and 1¼" circle templates, ¾" and 1¼" triangle templates, Mini Scallop scissors, Red and Black markers

Large Angel - ⅛" circle punch, ½" star punch, ¾" heart punch, ¾", ⅞" and 2" circle templates, 1¼" and 2⅛" triangle templates, Scallop and Jumbo Scallop scissors, Red and Black markers

Create festive holiday designs with Scallop, Pinking and Bow Tie scissors.

"A perfect package wrap for everyone."

Turn this...into ➔

Small Gifts - ½" circle template, ¾" x 1½" rectangle template, 1" square template, Mini Scallop, Mini Pinking and Bow Tie scissors

Large Gifts - ¾" circle template, ⅞" x 2" rectangle template, 1½" square template, Mini Scallop, Scallop, Pinking and Bow Tie scissors

"Frosty the cute and clever snowman is the perfect addition to any winter day."

Turn this...into ➔

Small Snowman - ⁷⁄₁₆" heart punch, ½" square template, ⅞" and 1¹⁄₁₆" circle templates, ¼" x ⅝" and ¼" x 1" strips, Mini Scallop scissors

Large Snowman - ¾" heart punch, ¾" square template, 1" and 1½" circle templates, ⁵⁄₁₆" x 1¼" and ⁵⁄₁₆" x 1½" strips, Scallop and Mini Pinking scissors

"Who's there? Boo, Boo Who."

Turn this...into ➔

Small Santa - ¼", ⁵⁄₁₆" and ⅝" circle punches, ⅝" circle template, 1¼" oval template, Mini Scallop and Scallop scissors

Large Santa - ¹⁵⁄₁₆" and ¾" circle punches, ⅜" and ¾" circle templates, 2" oval template, Scallop and Jumbo Scallop scissors

Wonderful Weaving

Woven paper adds texture and makes fabulous designs. Weave great colors together.

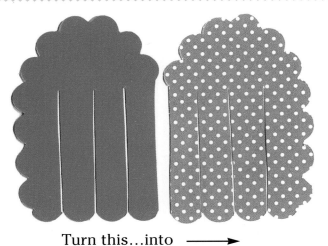

Turn this…into ➝

"Weave a simple heart with scallop edges."

Folk Heart - Jumbo Scallop scissors

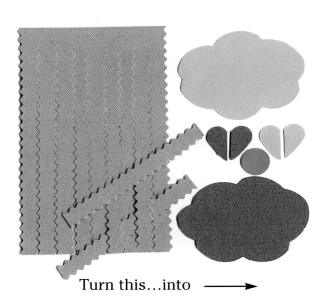

Turn this…into ➝

"Ice Cream and cake is perfect for parties."

Ice Cream Cone - $5/16$" circle punch, $7/16$" heart punch, $1\frac{1}{2}$" x $2\frac{1}{4}$" rectangle template, $1\frac{1}{4}$" oval template, Mini Pinking, Scallop and Cloud scissors (Glue woven strips together, then cut out the cone shape)

Turn this…into ➝

"Create a beautiful heart for any occasion."

Framed Heart - $1/16$" circle punch, $3\frac{1}{4}$" square template, $2\frac{3}{4}$", 3" and $3\frac{1}{4}$" heart templates, Jumbo Scallop scissors (Glue woven strips together then cut out the center heart shape.)

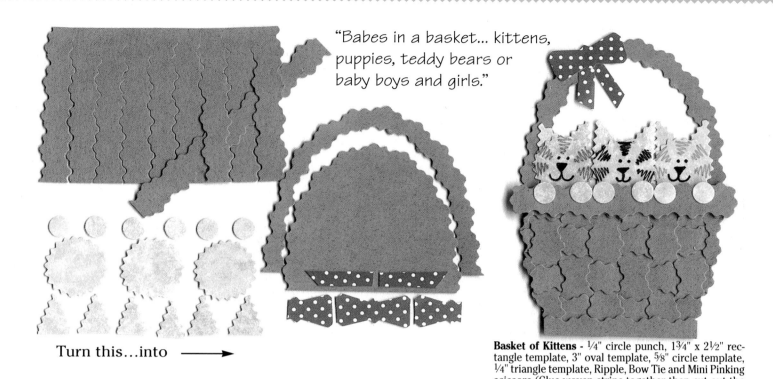

"Babes in a basket... kittens, puppies, teddy bears or baby boys and girls."

Turn this...into ➡

Basket of Kittens - ¼" circle punch, 1¾" x 2½" rectangle template, 3" oval template, ⅝" circle template, ¼" triangle template, Ripple, Bow Tie and Mini Pinking scissors (Glue woven strips together then cut out the basket shape.)

"Mom's famous homemade holiday pie. Make mine apple, pumpkin, peach, cherry, mincemeat or yummy pecan."

Apple Pie - ⅝" circle punch, 1⅜", 2¼", 2½" and 3" circle templates, Mini Pinking, Pinking and Scallop scissors (Glue woven strips together then cut them to fit behind the pie.)

Turn this...into ➡

Crimped Designs

"The perfect school girl smile."

Girl - 1¼" circle punch, 1¼" circle template, 1¼" heart template, Mini Scallop, Scallop, Jumbo Scallop and Bow Tie scissors, Crimper

Turn this...into ➔

"Crimping adds great texture to pine tree for winter scenes and holiday trees."

Turn this...into ➔

Pine Trees - ⅜" x 1" rectangle template, 1½" x 2½" triangle template, Scallop scissors, Crimper

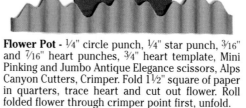

Turn this...into ➔

Flower Pot - ¼" circle punch, ¼" star punch, ³⁄₁₆" and ⁷⁄₁₆" heart punches, ¾" heart template, Mini Pinking and Jumbo Antique Elegance scissors, Alps Canyon Cutters, Crimper. Fold 1½" square of paper in quarters, trace heart and cut out flower. Roll folded flower through crimper point first, unfold.

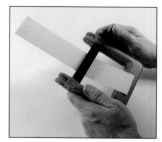

Crimping Paper - Use heavy cardstock paper. Simply roll it through the Tool for fantastic crimper results! You can also purchase crimped/corrugated paper.

"Palm trees and coconuts make any sandy beach scene complete."

Turn this…into ⟶

Palm Tree - ⅝" circle template, Deckle, Jumbo Scallop and Mini Pinking scissors, Crimper. Assemble tree, run through crimper. Crimp grass separately.

"Pine trees and pinecones are perfect for the holiday season."

Turn this…into ⟶

Pine Cones - 1⅛" and 1⅝" oval templates, Scallop and Mini Pinking scissors, Crimper

"Plant a pot with ivy."

Turn this…into ⟶

Ivy - ⅝" heart template, Mini Pinking scissors, Crimper

Showy Snowflakes

Use wavy-edge scissors to cut marvelous snowflakes! It is easy to make your own creative designs!

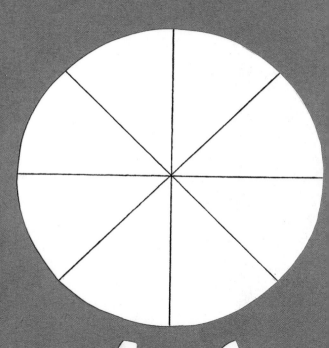

Snowflakes

Cut a 3" circle. Score along the fold lines making 8 equal sections. Fold in half then in half again. Transfer pattern to one quarter section. Cut design using required wavy edge scissors. Cut diamonds on outside edges. Open circle and refold into quarters placing uncut diamonds on outside edges. Cut remaining diamonds.

Diamond

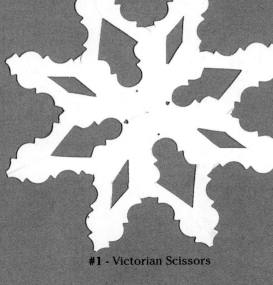

#1 - Victorian Scissors

 # 2 - Jumbo Antique Elegance Scissors

#3 - Provincial Scissors

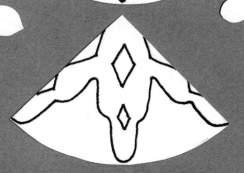

#4 - Wave Scissors

#5 - Jumbo Pinking Scissors

#6 - Victorian scissors

#7 - Jumbo Scallop Scissors

#8 - Scallop scissors

#9 - Bow Tie Scissors

#10 - Peaks scissors

OUR FAMILY

Ruth

Edwin

Dee

David

Debbie

Tim

Our Family - ¼" and ⅝" circle punches, ¾" and ⁷⁄₁₆" heart punches, ⁵⁄₁₆", ⅝", ⅞" and 1" circle templates, ¾" and 1" heart templates, ⅝" x 1¾" rectangle template, 2⅝" oval template, ¼" triangle template, Deckle, Cloud, Jumbo Wave, Mini Scallop, Jumbo Scallop, Mini Pinking and Bow Tie scissors, Alps Canyon cutters, 1" letter stickers

Template Shapes

Plastic templates are available in a wide variety of sizes and shapes. Use basic shapes such as hearts, circles, ovals and squares as building blocks to make just the right design for your scrapbook page or stationery. Place any plastic template on the wrong side of paper and trace the required shape with a pencil. Use straight scissors to cut around the shape leaving a border wide enough to allow for the use of wavy edge scissors. Place wavy edge scissors against the pencil line and cut the shape. As you cut, turn the paper, not the scissors. To avoid mistakes, practice on scrap paper.

Ivy Page - Sunflower and Jumbo Antique Elegance scissors, Alps Canyon cutters

Scenic Borders

*B*uild terrific borders for project backgrounds easily
with wavy edge scissors and colors of acid-free cardstock.*

Mountains - Deckle scissors, Alps Canyon cutters

Grass - Jumbo Deckle, Leaf, Peaks and Jumbo Scallop
scissors, Alps Canyon cutters

Snow - Alps Canyon cutters

Beach - Jumbo Wave, Wave, Jumbo Classic Wave
and Clouds scissors, Camel Back Canyon cutters

Sand - Jumbo Classic Wave scissors

Seaweed - Sunflower scissors